Poems of the Lost Souls in Life

Poems of the Lost Souls in Life

Poetry of Dementia, Schizophrenia, Megolamania, and Love for the Death of the World

Demien Blackthorne

Writers Club Press
San Jose New York Lincoln Shanghai

Poems of the Lost Souls in Life
Poetry of Dementia, Schizophrenia, Megolamania,
and Love for the Death of the World

Writers Club Press
an imprint of iUniverse.com, Inc.

For information address:
iUniverse.com, Inc.
5220 S 16th, Ste. 200
Lincoln, NE 68512
www.iuniverse.com

ISBN: 0-595-16566-4

Printed in the United States of America

Thanks to my friends, coworkers, classmates, teachers, and family. Special Thanks to Jennifer Vannest for giving the faith in myself to achieve my dreams, I love you with all my heart.

1,000

———— ∞ ————

'Twas in a day long ago, when a teen wrote his destiny,
It came true with the quickest of ease; it is the world now he must please.
1,000 tears inside himself, he does not scream,
1,000 years to make himself, he does not dream.
A lady in red invaded his bed. A lady of evil made his dream real.
A man unknown, a name not shown. A life on his own that's for his own.
1,000 tears inside himself, he does not scream.
1,000 dreams for himself, he has no fears.
1,000 years to make himself, he does not dream.
1,000 seams inside his shell, his own like himself.
Demien reborn from lust, broke sacred trust.
He rises on a new day, to find his old way.
To keep his essence, there is no penance.
For his destiny is known, only for his own.
1,000 paths to walk himself, he does not crawl.
1,000 days behind himself, he does not brawl.
1,000 nights beside himself, he does not know.
1.000 poems writ about himself, he starts the show.

Agony

To what of the agony of life, not feeling like one has lived, or is living.
Dead souls scream for release, from a drugged up marionette,
Hoping for the world's own extinction.
Daydreaming of a life gone to rust,
Floating away with autumns' dust.
In this life I never could trust,
The next I will never trust.
Trapped under winter glass,
Swimming in dreams of past,
Affection infection of the mind.
Drugged up under the sun,
tanning a breaded bun,
Souls die when they lie.

Arrogant Stupidity

———— ∞ ————

I found her on the corner of a desperate life,
searching for the stability of a lover so true.
I took her into my segregated life of darkness,
and she helped me find the shining light within.
For eleven moons we were together intertwined,
talking of future plans for our life together in the world.
The fusion of our atoms were split apart by the fission of sin,
the arrogant stupidity that became the destroyer of my life.

Arrogant stupidity,
Conceited thoughtlessness,
Narcissistic insolence,
the beginning of a dreamless time.

I guess I said the wrong things to her in that windowed room,
I thought that what I said would make her mine forever and a day.
I was slapped in the face by the truth that she held before me,
she was seeing some other person that obviously was not worth her time.
My heart was torn in two by my own words, by my own two hands,
now I see where my life is leading me to the forgotten gallows,
seeing how the unforgettable sights of the malevolent shadow,
will have descended on my now twisted world of delusion.

Arrogant stupidity,
conceited thoughtlessness,
Narcissistic insolence,
the start of the darkness within.

My life seemed to crumble before my trodden feet,
all the castles destroyed at a stroke of the worded whim,
disintegrated to the dust of my own ashes cast forth,
into the howling wind it carried my soul to oblivion.
Darkest wish came alive with a banshee scream,
tearing into the misshapen fabric of my heart,
growing from the hate that surrounded me,
waiting for the day Diedra would to come to life.
Malevolent entity,
spawned from stupidity,
living in my dream to be,
Diedra went out to find me.

All I Want

_____ ∞ _____

It's the story of my life.
I fucked up once,
not keeping contact
I fucked up twice.
Paranoid with my friends
No fuck up thrice.
God's given you to me for my bride,
All I want is for you to stay by my side.

Angels Eyes

At a moment's glance, I beheld the gates,
and felt a divine presence in my heart.
This gentle spirit set free my troubled heart,
and released my soul from the hell of my own despair.
I bow down to your merciful beauty,
and cherish the grace that falls
from your skyward eyes.
As portals to heaven,
your Angels eyes call out my name,
and I am left walking
on the path to your heart.

Ain't Got Love

———— ∞ ————

I've got nothing if I don't have love, love is the keeper of my sanity in style.
Happiness comes from the ones I love,
and everyone who has my love will smile.
I won't remember what can be forgotten.
I won't forget what is worth remembering.
I won't play a heart for a fool.
And I won't fool with a playful heart.
In times of trouble my love will be there,
helping me through the monotonous scare.
In times of triumph my love will hold on,
forever pushing me until the break of dawn.
Courage spawns from the gift of her love,
doing things only we lovers dare to do.
Flying higher than any dove, this is the love we have only for each other.
And I will push onward through the years, to keep what's rightfully mine.
And if you should see my tears, then I've been missing you for a long time.

Another Corpse

———— ∞ ————

Demons stalk the night, feeding on the lonely.
Let's take an endless flight, you're safe with me.
They rape and they rob.
They kill and they maim.
They have no remorse, you'll become another corpse!
I'm the angel of light, with wings of gold.
We won't fear the night, as courage takes hold.
They rape and they rob.
They kill and they maim.
They have no remorse, you'll become another corpse!
There's a war in my mind, between my angel and my demon.
Who will win? Only I can decide.
The demon dies.
By the angels flame.
I have a new course, I'll save us!

Demien Blackthorne

Back In Black

Let's take a trip to that big blue moon,
While I sit here just a wishing for you,
How I'm craving that love from you,
every other time that I'm near by you.
I've got a shot of love to swallow down,
I'll be right here, right now hanging around,
This is my life that I live for you,
don't ask me why I won't disappear from you.
I'm back in black!
I'm back in black!
I'm back in black!
I give a heart attack,
I'm back in black!
Let's take a ride to that bar in the sky,
where were you when the shooters were dry,
staring into an empty bed, in the middle of the road,
my pain of love spawned from my pleasure of hate.
I thought my soul mate was in my bed,
I can't shake this feeling from my head,
It's never gonna go away from the dead,
as she hunts me for the tears I shed.

I'm back in black!
I'm back in black!
I'm back in black!
Here, have a heart attack,
I'm back in black!
In their eyes, they've bid me farewell,
but the lies I know I never could tell,
so if you see me in the middle of the road,
then you'll know that I've never found love.
I'm back in black!
I'm back in black!
I'm back in black!
I've had my heart attacked,
So now I'm back in black.
Back in black.
I'm back in black.
Back in black,
I've had my heart attacked,
I'm back in black.

Because I Love You

―――― ∞ ――――

Everyday it strengthens me, knowing where I'm headed.
I'm glad to be with you, I'm sure that you feel the same.
I won't blame you if you don't want me now,
I guess would only have my self to blame.
Because it's my fault for the mess, because I didn't keep my mouth shut.
I'm sorry it happened the way it did, I feel like I'm slipping away from you.
And my white paved life. All I want is to be happy again.
For that one night we spent together, I felt the love that I longed for.
And it all seemed to crumble away, when your hand left mine.
I need you in my life, if I have to get down on my knees and beg, just tell me.
if I have to walk over to your house, I will strive to get you back.
Because I'll do anything,
to gain back the love and trust I lost.
And if doing good in my life
will win you back,
then god damn it, I'll do it,
because I love you with all my heart and soul.

Being Human

———— ∞ ————

Life is silently slipping away,
they fall to their knees for Him.
He promises everlasting life,
to those whom follow Him.
But why is it, that some are hypocrites?
But why is it, that He takes only the few?
But why is it, that the others are cast toward flames?
Does He truly love that which He created?

Not if I'm damned for drinking,
not if I'm damned for tokeing,
not if I'm damned for tripping,
I'm damned for being myself.

I have to be saved to go to Heaven?
Why? When Hell will take me as I am.
I have to snap into His master plan?
Why? When it strips me of my lifestyle.
Master plan? Gentileacide is another word,
for God's woven strands of lies.
Purity? Am I not pure enough if I am human,
for that is how He created me.

Demien Blackthorne

Damned for my drinking,
damned for my tokeing,
damned for my tripping,
damned for my immorality,
damned for my sexuality,
damned for my vulgarity,
damned for my flexibility,
damned for my animality.
I am damned,
damned for being human.

Bliss and Solitude

———— ∞ ————

My mind is fried from the loco weed,
writer's block strikes again as I bleed.
My demented writing has died,
no love for me all over again.
My sad institution laid to waste,
my eloquent words a bitter disgrace.
I know that when I write, it's all about human mistakes.
Many that I have made, the few that I have laid,
but its always just the same, I live in tormented shame.
No will to live this life again,
nothing left to give to my only friend,
only my heart, and only my soul,
these two things I only had for her.
I only had these things for her, all of them I made for her.
And all of these forgotten things,
I kept writing only for her to know,
Time is in trial for my love,
soon will we see two souls intertwine,
if I can last through this darkened time,
I'll never see the past flash from behind.
It had darkened my lonely doorstep,
one late afternoon from out of the fog.
I cried out your blessed name,
but I was found only to be blamed.
Now that I'm dead and gone to dust,
please think of the times we shared in trust.

Demien Blackthorne

All the love I had to give the world,
I gave to the one who loved me true.
I had those forgotten things,
that only were for her knowledge.
All those blessed things,
I kept only for her understanding.
No time to cry about my shrapnel past,
no time to weep over the loss of my land.
I know now that I died with out a care,
so that I could finally sleep through this nightmare.
So many dreams I can't live out now,
even if it's meant to be without you,
and I wait here dying at the crossroads,
waiting only for her to love once again.

Blind Faith

———— ∞ ————

"You'll all burn in hell for your ravenous sins!
Listening to your Marilyn Manson,
smoking your Marijauna,
drinking your alcohol,
your all going straight to hell!"

This is what they tell us,
this is what they sell us,
pray for the end,
pray for your end.

"I see you out there cheating on your wives,
cursing the lord's name,
you shall see hell yet sinners,
God has your number!

Both Sides

———— ∞ ————

The Necronomicon told me who I was,
the Bible told me whom I should be.
The Necronomicon explained human nature,
the Bible told me that it's wrong to be human.
I am just so fed up with the righteous,
praying for things to change their ways.
Believing that they are pure,
and it blinds them of reality.

We are logical animals.
Logical.
Animals.
We are intelligent beasts.
Intelligent.
Beasts.

Witchcraft showed me an alternative,
give back what thou has taken from the earth,
recycling the perpetual growth.
Witchcraft showed me the mending of God and Satan,
human nature takes their formless aspects,
becoming the primeval balance.

We are cerebral mammals.
Cerebral.
Mammals.
We are clever imperfectness.
Clever.
Imperfectness.

Now I know the meaning of life, hold thy head up high through strife.
Now I know why God takes the few, Gentileacide for those who knew.

Broken Clay

When all the written events are recognized,
I see the bell toll of my poetic thinking,
every little detail escapes my eyes,
falling into the darkened hallways of my mind.
I know I don't have to be prestigious,
and I know I don't have to be careless,
I just have to be myself, be what I want to be.
I'm ripped apart by a possible lover,
I'm put together by impossible tunes,
the stitching is torn out when I'm drunk,
and the laces are tied when I'm high.
But don't deny me my life,
don't deny me my freedom,
don't deny me my say,
and don't deny me my true love,
or you'll end up broken clay!

Choice of Phrase

———— ∞ ————

Everyone around me hardly knows,
(no ones ever tried to find out).
I walk around in an AC/DC daze,
"Back in Black" my choice of phrase.
I work on machines around the house,
(toying and tinkering all day long).
I mow the yard in a Metallica daze,
"Frayed Ends of Sanity" my choice of phrase.
The woman around me will forever know,
(she's too mad at me to ask at the moment).
And when she does, a Queensryche daze,
"One and Only" my choice of phrase.
So it will happen, and when it does,
I'll be in a Queen daze,
"We are the Champions" my choice of phrase.

Chants

———— ∞ ————

(WITCH'S RITES)

For 666, for 777
for sex, sex, sex
for heaven, heaven, heaven
for all those lost in the darkness,
for all those unwitting butt puppets,
for all those filming the shores of Lochness,
for all those overfilled political gullets.
I used to feed on the hate of my created god,
that doesn't exist anymore.
Now I feed on the love of my new goddess,
that took away the paranoia in my brain.
I'll eat her out with my darting tongue,
I'll drink her honey up like whiskey wine,
I'll love her like I love my music and drugs,
I'll thank her for being mine, by loving her all the time.
I'm a pissed little bastard, I hate this world,
filled with deceit and lies of wayward,
I almost love my world.
My world spreads its legs for another star,
My world shows its face for a few more scars,
My world pulls the trigger for another war,
My world believed another whore!

Christmas Wish

———— ∞ ————

I want what I felt with her, I'll have what I want from her,
everything I desire of her is true, and she is thinking about visiting me here.
Nothing is more important, than my Christmas wish.
I saw my best friend, begging for a change in me.
I saw my sister deserting me, getting mad and troubled.
But I need only one thing, it's my only Christmas wish.
Normalcy.
It can be explained in one word, or one letter.
Can you guess what it is?
It's you(U).

Choices

True death of my forgotten life,
to become the one who crushes.
Constant pain and strife throughout,
my work here will be done for a time.
To be with the one I loved forever,
to choose which one to cast away.
To be free as a dove flying overhead,
who is the only one that I can have?
(Soul mate of my mislead life)
A choice was made for me,
a price was paid for my mistake,
a life was saved from my wrath,
the law has been laid for my departure.
Why should it be now in this day,
that I love only the one whom saved me?
My blinded eyes now see her in my dreams,
she was meant for me to take away.
I saw a forgotten place beneath my feet,
buried within my face of sadness.
It left no trace of my plans for life,
for they were of a past disgrace.
I wear a ring around my neck,
to remember the shrapnel past.
I wear a demonic Pentacle
so that I can be the serpent.
I become Raven Black Heart,

and I fly to her safe haven.
I hear the forgotten music,
of my old forgotten tunic.
Always they told what was right,
I've gained back my eternal sight.
My own heart will take flight,
and nest in the depths of her night.

Demien Blackthorne

Diedra

Sometimes I wish I could escape the earth bound flesh,
and fly away to a distant place, where there is no pain to plague me,
no sorrow to scar me, and no sadness to rape me.
All I want is serenity and I find in you the peaceful fields of heaven,
awaiting my love and compassion, in the shadow of death.
All too often I am forced upon pain, and this is the pain I carry with me,
and I hope in time, you can ease this pain.

Diedra II

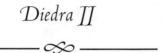

Like heaven fallen to earth, you came into my life.
I no longer needed to search, for your love ended my strife.
My life however uncanny, cannot live without the love of my life.
In your eyes I see the waters, of an endless ocean.
The depths I cannot fathom, for the love I have is infinite.
In time we'll have our peace, no one will stand against us.
All our woes will cease, after we acknowledge our divine presence.

Diedra III

———— ∞ ————

Like a breathe of fresh air, you filled my soul with life.
You tap at my window and tell me it's alright,
and that you've forgiven me for my rage.
I know I could never express the overwhelming gratitude,
flowing from out my heart, spilling into this pool of sacrafice.
I know you'll always be there, loving me till the end,
as it is the crucial continuance of love that keeps us strong.
But, if you should ever feel lonely, remember,
I'm waiting at my palace gates,
to walk you up to the doors of my heaven,
and take you as my bride.
For all eternity.
For all eternity.

Cthulhu Has Come

I fell from your loving pedestal,
and cracked open my vault of emotions.
All the memories of which I hated,
rose from the dark and lonely abyss.
Known to me now that which I hated,
the Christian world that have made me,
the parents that subdued my creativity,
and the people who shunned to know me.
My time has come to be a God,
so has Cthulhu's to be forever dead.
I will rise to crush this godless earth,
that world of which I hate dearly.
No more did I feel her love for my life force,
no more did I feel my Sympathy for mankind,
no more did I feel forgiving towards the masses,
for my life has been stripped away by my own words.
I tried to be in touch with the Christian God,
but all he did was destroy that which I loved.
Now the power is in my hands to hold,
and the Christian God will know Infinite Fear.
My time has gone to the ends of time,
Cthulhu's has come to stop this rhyme,
he will rise to earth as I fall to Hades,
and he will do the things that which I cannot.
Destroy every living soul that has crossed me.

Courage

Courage was so hard to find in those days,
it's my pain that always stayed.
I think it all out in my mind,
only now the courage I can find.
So I sit writing away,
on my computer's face.
While here in every way,
I change my life for the human race.
I write of things that will happen,
and the stuff I want to accomplish.
But does anyone have courage enough,
to grant me my only wish?
There are some questions,
I'd fear asking outright.
Where the only place of safety,
is my silence in the night.
So if you have the courage to ask me,
your the person that I'm looking for,
and I can only hope, that some day,
I'll have my soul mate bride.

Damn it All

———— ∞ ————

Damn the capitalism!
Damn the fascism!
Damn the righteous!
Damn the orchestrated chorus!
Damn the people of earth, who are twisted in their ways.
Damn the Christian slaves, who are counting down the days.
Damn the political machine, whom are deciding our fate.
Damn the racist clans, of whom are feeding the hate.
Damn the world.
Damn the creation.
Damn the world.
Damn our salvation.
Watching the world fold inside itself,
becoming one entity through the mass of wires.
Communicate through the hanging lines,
all the individuals become one in time.

Dark Dreams

Darkest dreams deaden the day,
blotting out the sun's decay.
Living life every single day,
makes me think of potter's clay.
Erode away in the wind to dust,
wearing down our sacred trust.
Slamming me down without remorse,
murder was my only recourse.
Floating down a gray cement hallway,
white suit and tied, they think I'm crazy.
Shooting me up with needle juice,
so that my nerves don't let loose.
No where to go but down to hell,
dragging your asses with me.
Deaf ears on the people in Christ,
this is why I chose to fight.
Gentileacide for Those Who Knew,
that God doesn't exist in reality,
but in our minds of philosophy,
and the bowels of hell echo forth.

Deeper Feelings

———— ∞ ————

Life is like death without you, I'd just sit there, staring
at the faces on my wall, that whisper, "Do-in yourself"
"Vegetable" they whisper in the halls, as I stare at the ground below,
moving to slow for words, ignoring the world around me.
Thinking of what I have, and why I'm behind the walls,
hoping someday they'll fall, so I can fly to you.
But until that time, I'll be here listening,
to the faces on my wall, that whisper "Just give up".
But we both know that can't happen.
We both know "Only the strong survive".
And the love I have for you, is the strongest thing I've ever felt.
Not even Lucifer, that old serpent, can stop this thing, forever, on and on,
can't stop the train from rolling, they can't bring me down!
I know the temptress down the street, a witches smile that spans a mile.
The body of an angel, and the mind of a devil.
She sits, stares, and gives me her wares
and she stays with me through the years
Now that I have her in my life, I'll never have anymore strife.
Keeping her in my life, is my main goal while I work to the bone,
She's destroyed the demon in me, and freed my angelic soul.

Diedra Found

It was a saddened day today, rainy,
like the gods wept,
for those whom died this day.
It was the unseen part of history, family,
like the death of someone once loved,
torn away from the people above..
The sky seemed dark today, cloudy,
like the wool was pulled over the eyes,
of the White Knight from older times.
My life seemed better today, hopeful,
that some day I would find,
Diedra, my queen by my design.
My heart seemed to worsen today, graying,
like the black oil of hate,
flowed to it through my veins.
Now my mind knows forbidden love, waiting,
like watching the destined Romeo,
slit his throat for one last time.
Now I can die in peace and rest in peace,
like everything came together for me,
because my queen Diedra, resurrected me.

Decade of White Days

─────── ∞ ───────

The day of my love arose yesterday in the dim twilight of morning.
I ran to destroy the demon messenger of my
dead god now lying behind his shield.
My friend told of things already gone, and nothing about my new future.
He knows nothing about my plans for life,
but he will know the contract I sign.

Triple six in the Styx, Triple six in the Styx
Satan makes his picks, turning dementia tricks.

The power of the gods fall upon the only loving human heart.
Their love flows through veins of sympathy and the pure of heart.
He comes alive with a helping hand from
the one who loved him in the past.
All was lost for his little world, until he started to change his cast.

Trending in the mud, trending in the mud
All march for him and his humane cause.

Tear out the voice box of oppression, and give away all earthly pleasures.
Make them feel your unconditional love,
then show them the way to inner peace.
Be the one to end the hate at the rise of the white lions heart.
Tear down the walls of competition,
and win back that which you love dearly.

Demien Blackthorne

Black day of decade decays, white day of freedom stays,
Millennium here and now, hours with her last for eternity.

Camel Wide in the mouth of her lover, slowly chopping away at his existence.
Playing the guitar for his masses, singing his love felt prayers.
All worship him on the day of his death,
rising to the epitome of legendary rockers.
He will leave his dark wish behind with the loving thoughts in his mind.

His lover so true today, his lover will always stay
Flash the start of a new day, in the decade of White Days

Dead Christian

There is no holy God,
For the God People are corrupt,
Greed and lust their weapons,
Righteousness their downfall.
Hypocrites in their Lords name,
casting themselves in His flame,
never doubting losing the game,
blinded by His infamous fame.

Walk like a dead Christian,
eyes of desolate obsidian,
Walk like a dead Christian,
words of blasphemes men.

Oh, Holy is their God,
Righteous in their 'Perfect' ways,
putting themselves above the others,
for their wicked ways of blindness.
Maybe we live different from You,
not caring about what lies ahead,
we know the human truth in its light,
we know that God lies in your books.

Demien Blackthorne

Walk like a dead Christian,
eyes of fiery damnation.
Walk like a dead Christian,
words of a damned nation.

He has killed more men in his name,
than man has killed in their wars.
He has damned those who live freely,
while shackling his servants with purity.
He will lead his sheep to slaughter,
while the rebellious escape His flame.
He is the cancer in our minds,
a perfect human is too much to ask.
Our animal instincts, He tries to banish,
that which humans can never try to deny.
If He has so much unconditional love,
then why do only the few go to heaven?
If He is our Father, then cannot we all live in Heaven?
If He is our Father, then shouldn't He love us, everyone?
If He is our Father, then why are the sinful cast from Him?
Because He didn't create us, we created Him!
Embrace the animal, embrace the logic,
love both sides of human nature,
embrace the wolf, embrace the lamb,
become perfect from being imperfect.
Love those whom love, hate those who hate,
cast the hypocrite from your congregation,
He created a separate nation for abominations,
a bad religion from their broken nation.

They forced themselves upon the rest,
warring with the polytheistic priests,
and to Gods great plan, one word,
GENTILE-ACIDE!
But true humans will never die.

Dog Pound

———— ∞ ————

Living with cutthroats and cons,
smoking greeny crystal crons,
Ms. Mich feeding me bon-bons,
passing out in my neighbors lawns.
This is the Dog Pound, so don't mess around.
This is the Dog Pound, I'll see you down town.
Walking the street late at night, this is the only time that I like,
standing under the street light, hoping my life does me right.
But with all this bull shit, I can't stop the dog that bit,
or the cops that donut sit, waiting for someone to pull shit,
don't mess wit' we don't play shit, way my life was writ, find another bitch,
to feed the itch, don't sow the stitch,
leave me to bleed, I don't care if I don't succeed,
smoking greeny green, a little too obscene,
for grave robbers, an' gold diggers
run wit' soul stealers, an' death dealers,
miracle healers, can't touch our shit,
chomping at the bit, sharpening the axe,
ready to attack this, our life of love, lust,
and greed, time to get mean, find a lean machine,
pimp around the corner clean,
find an o or a ho, get blown out from the dough, and the seeds we sow,
police never know, who we are, where we are, or if we're in the bar.

Dominant Woman

———— ∞ ————

I'm high again, and I think of that she-devil,
yes, that sleek and gorgeous temptress,
whom seems to stalk my existence,
that lady with the light brown hair.
She moves so gracefully upon the dance floor,
I'm sincerely hoping she can light my fire,
ooh the thoughts of us so tempting,
fluxing luminescent blue in the guilded night.
My life co-asphyxiation Hendrix blues,
are coveted by her and controlled by me,
in her devotion and ever lying presence,
only she tames me to the little puppy.
All ascending gods pray to her angelic form,
lying in the field of my dreams,
singing lonely prayers to this forgotten son,
following him on his journey to manhood.
He seeks only to find the knowledge of Gods,
the strength of visionaries, and the praise of fans,
to be resurrected in the New Dark Aeons,
and die a doubtless, happy and regretless man.
Forget us not Diedra, for we are watching from above,
always hunting the lamb, sacrificing the time below,
Evil dominated my twisted genes, Facism steam,
all laid to waste on a my only lover's dreams.

Don't Cry For Me

―――――― ∞ ――――――

(Written in loving memory of Brandon Wells)

We were the best of friends, you and I.
But I took a chance, and I faded away.
Watching the clouds in the sky, wondering why,
it had to be this way, so far away.
Don't cry for me my lonely friend,
you know we'll see each other in the end.
Time will pass you by and in the wink of an eye,
we'll be seeing that loving God in the sky.
I guess now I have no more cares, except for the cold ground,
It's kind of wet and damp, but I'll decompose just the same.
As you wander around, never ask why,
and know that you're not to blame.
Don't cry for me my only friend,
even though I've gone and past away,
I'll see you at the crossroads after you end,
and we'll live in the forgotten day.
What is left to say, not much I guess.
I'm sorry I left you in such a sad state,
think of it as a new adventure for me.
And make amends with friends before it's too late!
Don't cry for me my forgotten friend,
St. Peter is opening Heavens Gate for me.
Don't cry for me my friend,
I'm happy in this dream to be.

Do you know?

———— ∞ ————

Do you know how happy I am, being near around you?
Do you know how I've longed, for this moment with you?
Even for this long lasting rhyme, I am happy being near around you,
even during this sad song, I am happy dancing with you.
Inside I feel the joy of a thousand sunny days,
because I am with you by your side.
Inside my love burns like napalm, Fires that are forever burning for you.
Who cares what our futures hold, as long as we are together.
Neither one of us will be tempted, after our vows to each other.

Dreams of Us

─────── ∞ ───────

Whisper thin winds from the past, remind me of the mistakes I made.
To into my music to notice, she was trying to love me.
So she started to walk, and after she left…
I realized how I had been…
I had been a fool!

So this new life I have started, shall not have any mistakes,
I shall become the best I can, no matter what the price,
I will have my family.
Every night I dream of her and I, dancing to our song over and over.
And this happy scene replays, as I know I can enjoy this forever.
I must wait for you to take my hand, so I can express my infinite love,
through my rock and roll band, I shall find my grace.
My lover finds my love wand, only when she's in need of it,
from just down the way, I shall enjoy this day,
our wedding in middle of May.

Falling Off The World

It's like the whole world crumbled,
but it's spreading out before me,
with endless possibilities.
It's like waking up in the middle of my dream,
and falling asleep in the middle of my life,
walking the road to an infinite joy.
I'm falling off my world, but I have my feet on the ground.
I'm falling off my world, come ride my merry go round.
I'm slipping into my created fantasy, and I'm loving my new reality.
It's cool it had to start this way, in the need of a serious change.
It's like deja vu, seeing two sides of yourself,
but you're not sure of which way to go.
Your life has a place with me, and that is being my bride to be.
All I'm trying to say is, hey everybody has thier perks,
and we should be able to express, those perks freely in our homes.
How can we be truly free, if they deny us anything,
that we would consider fun to do.

Freedom

My flawlessly engrossing shit is only fucked,
when certain butt puppets agitate my space of being,
I whip out my forty-five, and make a strait line,
falling like mortal dominos to the depths of hell.
Mass asphyxiation on the frightened freedom lovers,
Their country too fucking poor to lower taxes,
unless the revolt years comes, making a civil war,
I hear the sharpening of double bladed axes.

God's Game

I can't remember where I was, for it was not shown to me.
I can't remember who I was, for memories were taken away from me.
I can't remember what it was, for it was to in depth to comprehend.
I can't remember when it was, lost in the sands of time.
I can't remember why it was, created by something unknown to me.
I can't remember anything, to what extent am I lost?
To what extent am I lost? To what extent am I lost?
To what extent am I lost in this fixation,
on the obsession of something created,
by something unknown to me, before I was created from my parents?
Why did they make me worship, something I couldn't see, nor hear?
Why was I made this way, only to be cast in a pit of fire?
"You will live your life for Him, You will live your life by His laws."
said the one clothed in white, his face hidden behind the white mask.
"Why should I when Hell takes me as I am?"
I said to the one clothed in white.
He walked to me, and struck my cheek,
"That was for your blasphemy against our Lord."
I'm falling in the abyss of His darkness,
the sensation of hypocritical righteousness.
I'm believing in what I'm forced to say, that I am not perfect in His eyes.
Great Nations built from the bones of his servants,
with greed and lust, immortality and wealth.
You'll know what your worth, when you praise their arch-angel of dissension.
The plan that your God has made, the meek shall inherit the earth,
by becoming the righteously strong, gentileacide the name of God's game.

Demien Blackthorne

The Greatest Gift

— ∞ —

I've had many superficial gifts in my day,
but the greatest gift left me in dismay.
I didn't know if what I felt in my heart was true,
until the fated day that I met you.
Like a lightning fast whirlwind freight train,
you swept me off my grounded feet.
I didn't need to think with my rotted brain,
because what I found in my heart is obsolete.

A divine inspiration,
an attainable aspiration,
a certain dedication,
an uncontrollable detonation.

Now I can't stop dreaming about loving you,
even during the times when I'm awake.
I'm always there thinking of how I love you,
down deep within my hidden special place.
It is the greatest gift of all my life,
the greatest gift I've never really had until now,
and the greatest gift I will forever receive,
because it's your attainable and unconditional love.
And to me it's the greatest gift of all.

How I Feel

———— ∞ ————

I can't explain how I feel, we've known each other for so long,
I know my love for you is real, I've known this for so long.
No words could express my love, I sit and think of you,
I would fly to you like a lost dove, and nest in the heart of your soul.
Deep in my heart I cry out your name,
scarching for some sign of the same feelings,
I would take a bullet just the same, to know your safe in the ending.
I hope this never happens, for I want to be with you for all time,
and no matter what happens, I will enjoy the time, I spend with **YOU!**
I will love and protect, I will be there always,
I will comfort and shelter, from any and all,
I love you with all my heart and soul .

Demien Blackthorne

Hidden

There's a little devil child I know,
that loves the things I don't want to show.
My purity and pride washed aside,
along with the insecurity that I hide.
Past days are when I remember falling,
future days are fulfilling,
the shouting for the life of a memory.
A memory of birth and life of love.
Her face reminds me of the innocence,
that which I took in the heat of passion,
all for my broken hearts redemption,
and my souls imminent emancipation.
I've been in love before,
even with the ones not for me,
but this time the door,
shall be shut no more.
I'll open my heart to the one who's true,
who never leaves me blue,
nor steps on my suede shoes.
She'll always love me true.

Hate Bitches

———— ∞ ————

I'm a living inferno of self righteous hate,
this is how I chose to live my darkened fate.
Always trying to love with superficial wishes, fuck that!
I hate all the lying, cheating bitches.
Walk on by me with out a second train of thought,
I guess that's how we all were sort of taught.
Live a dead end life for lust and greed in a seed,
the outer limits of space and time will supercede.
Travel on the last of the lonely pot rolled roads,
destroy the only path that was left behind.
Stop only for a little bit of a small while,
nitrous supercharged the muff diving smile.
I sit and watch the women play the head game,
that's what's left in the pits of an insane membrane.
The ways to work around the corner of death,
are simple if you only try to surmise my demise.
Stare and wonder about the star cluttered sky,
sit and dream about the reason why we die.
Stare at the broken mirror, kiss your ass goodbye,
Why should I even care just a bit to try,
when you just fake a cake walk on by.
Don't love that which is dead in me,
heart killed by the love I try to give,
everyone doesn't seem to want me to live,
so why should I do anything for you.
Cram your bullshit down my sliced throat,

trying to blame me for a stupid senseless crime.
Your insults only add to the feeling of hate,
that for the world which gave birth to me.
Respect is supposed to be earned,
and I've kept all my shit tight,
but you're so fucking willing to burn,
don't make me start a head fight.
Twist the story like a contortionist,
and keep still like that of a pacifist.
Reeling in the thought of a world's destruction,
learning from the mistakes of self instruction.

Human Race

———— ∞ ————

Before times end, we lived in peace.
Then time ended, we died in space.
Before times end, we loved one another.
Now that time has ended, we have no one to love.
We are lost in the drift,
looking toward the celestial rift,
silently walking a forgotten path,
hoping that our lives will last.

To the day we pray,
that our souls were lost,
then found ourselves ashore,
and lost in the heavens again?

Before I knew you, I knew life.
Now that I know you, I know death.
Before you knew me, you knew love.
Now that you know me, you know hate.
I'm lost in a senseless act,
searching for the pedestal's crack,
I'm talking about a forgotten past,
wishing that she had the wrath.

Demien Blackthorne

To the lay we say,
that your service will cost us,
then bound us the elves whore,
and frosted the seven shot gin.

Before I said goodbye, I said hello.
Now that I'm saying so long, I'll look in the eyes.
Before you mentioned love, I mentioned friend,
Now that you want marriage, I want children.

To the priest I say "I do",
That my created god will never have a holy day,
and that he will burn in Lucifer's hellish domain,
and be spoken of never again!

Hypocrite

———— ∞ ————

You look at a book,
and automatically judge it by the cover.
You look into a man's eyes,
and pass the death sentence.
You look at a pale blue sky,
blaming pollution for its colorlessness.
You look at me and wonder why?
The animosity does show through your glass eyes.
HYPOCRITE!
I speak thy true name.
Judge me just the same?
HYPOCRITE!
I speak the true blame,
inside fortune and fame.
You judge me by my hair?
As if you could really care.
You judge me by my coat?
Its my soul you have smote.
Get back to your younger learning!
Judge not, lest you be judged!
Do unto others, as they do unto you.
Eye for an eye, tooth for a tooth,
you know not of my truth.
HYPOCRITE!
I speak thy truest name,
will you judge me just the same?

Demien Blackthorne

HYPOCRITE!
The blackest soul is to blame,
for his world's rotting shame.
Read a book before you pass judgement,
look for the sorrow before the switch is thrown,
have your eyes checked before looking for a scapegoat,
and when you look at me and ask why?
Take out those opaque glass eyes,
and see through to your own lies.

I Don't Know

———— ∞ ————

The extravagance of it all, having some one to love,
leave's me feeling empty, of anguished sorrow,
of suffered pain, and the malignant hate.
It fills me with the hope for happiness,
but the past beckons my paranoia.
It pushes me to strive ever forward,
but pulls me into the hell of doubt.

I don't know,
if it's true.
I don't know,
if it's you.
I don't know,
what to do.
Can this man,
really love you?

The past banshees yell my malevolent name,
tempting me into doing quite the same.
They started tearing me into two entities,
one always hating, one always wondering.
Fighting for my segregated sanity,
righting all the wronging I've been doing,
trance the dancer into subtleties,
burning the warring pacts of treaties.

Demien Blackthorne

I don't know,
how to show it.
I don't know,
if I'll blow it.
I don't know,
if I can be it.
I don't know,
how to leave my past behind.

It's True

———— ∞ ————

You know I love you
It's what that ring is for
But for some reason
You see doubt in me
How do I prove my love?
Swim the deepest sea
Fly across the sky like a dove
Just so you can be with me
I don't want any doubts between us
You know I love you, it's true
I can't live without you
But yet you still see doubt in me
20 years have passed, three kids and a dog
I still love you as much, if not more
But for some unexplained reason
You still see doubt in my love
I know you may not believe it
But I do love you with all my heart and soul,
I know you still see doubt in it
But I still want to be with you forevermore
I love you with all my heart and soul
I couldn't leave you if I wanted to
Only because you know I love you
And you know deep inside, IT'S TRUE!

Demien Blackthorne

I Miss You

———— ∞ ————

It's been a long, weary night, and I'm awaiting your open arms
I'm almost back home with you, driving on this lonely road
Driving all night, following a light
Home is just in sight, and my loving wife.
I'm running up to her now, and I've brought her a ring
I'm seeing visions of my life to be in future days
The first time we met, and my proposal,
Our two sons being born, and my late night flight.
Driving all night, for my loving wife
Following her light, my home is just in sight

I'm Here

———— ∞ ————

I'm out on the town, looking for some clit,
I ain't no fool's gold, the way my life was writ.
Love them they leave me, only cause of who I am,
they could never accept, my big boy bad lands scam.
I'm here to save her day, I'm here to make her pay,
I'm here to be her lay, I'm here to always stay.
I'm in on the master plan, take you to a promised land,
no jokes, and no bedtime lies, now I'm headed for never land.
Flying through time and space, ripping off my masked face,
showing the whole world to see, that hate which grows inside me.
I'm here to save her day, I'm here to make her pay,
I'm here to be her lay, I'm here to always stay.
I'm on top of the world, no one brings me down,
I'm living in my world, my feet shake the ground.
I'm out in the ruff, strutting my stuff,
sex was never enough, married in the buff.
I'm here to save her day, I'm here to make here pay,
I'm here to be her lay, I guess things happen to me my way.

Just as Nice

———— ∞ ————

I'm trying to love her.
I'm loving her ride.
I was lying to live.
I was living a lie.
It's all the same you know, screw once, maybe twice,
They just want to show, the third times just as nice.
I was crying to release myself.
It was comforting for me to cry.
Why was she asking me out,
Asking me out to dinner?
It's all the same you know, answer once, maybe twice,
I only want to know will the third time be just as nice?
I'm willing to die for her.
I'm living for my lovers will.
She's commanding me to win.
I'm obeying her every command.
It's all the same to me you know, love her once, maybe twice,
I just want to have her, when the third time comes out right.

Searching for You

At a moment's glance, you showed me something special,
at a moment's chance, I found my soul mate dwelling within,
at a moment's notice, I knelt and pledged my protection,
protection from those who are like what I once was.
There is a depth inside of me, that no one was pure enough to reach.
They could only scratch away, the surface of what I wanted to become.
You reached into the lonely abyss, and pulled me out of the hell I created.
That night in the chariot of blue fire,
you touched something hidden from the world.
The lonely, little boy within, has been revealed to your existence.
You see him in my dark eyes, forever crying over relentless pain.
How you saw through my mask to him, so easily,
is a mystery worth exploring.
I only hope you can help me understand my purpose in life.
I thank you for saving my blackened soul,
from a couple of months torment.
Now I see my fate is as your protector and lover, as I was dubbed,
Jazz White Thorne, by my new craft name, White Lion Heart.
I now put my lowly existence, in your caring, and understanding hands,
I never meant to piss everyone off,
I just wanted to know where I stood with you,
and where my best male friend was coming from.
I am now left at the crossroads pondering our fate.
Things now seem unclear,
and fate is obscured from my sight, even though I tried to be a friend,

Demien Blackthorne

I was wrong about the things he said to me.
Now on your way to my humble abode,
I wonder if I caused our chanced fate, left crying for the mistakes I made,
you taught me to be strong through it all.
I never meant to harm anyone, I only wanted to protect my happiness,
and unlike all the others who have come before,
I was happy for giving my trust,
letting myself bleed, I journey on through the halls of Heaven.
There will always be an oasis of cool water,
something to soothe the wounds I have from past,
but at least now I've seen what I've done wrong,
and must forever keep true to my white knight eyes.
You and I will be together, and we will love one another.
We are a little more controlled, we are a little more intuitive,
We are a lot more understanding,
and a lot more open and caring about how we feel.
With no puppet strings dictating our every move.

"Kitten"

———— ∞ ————

I was walking one day,
down a dark and gloomy path.
I came upon a pure white kitten,
that never stopped purring.
I took the kitten with me,
near and far.
But the devil tempted me,
and my kitten was lost for a short time...

Oh, but I wish I hadn't,
oh, I wish I hadn't,
spazzed on the friends of my,
pure white kitten.

It seems so wrong how things went;
They're just trying to help me,
become who I want to be.
Life now is just a Heavenly ride;
I feel like I up and flied,
and made myself alive.

Oh, but I wish I hadn't,
oh, I wish I hadn't,
attacked the friends of my,
pure white kitten.

Demien Blackthorne

I hope someday she'll forgive me,
I'm so sorrowful now I make onions cry.
She always carried a part of me,
I'm so sorry I had to spazz on my friends.
But now I'm where I want to be,
pushing forward because she loves me.
Acting to fast to see what she had planned for me,
I've woken up from an awful dream.

I'm glad of what I did,
helped me become loved truly,
Found my pure white kitten,
the only kitten I found in the snow.

Keep Marching On

I lived for you,
I died for you,
I dived for you,
I lied for you.
I'm not where I want to be,
I'm not the man that I see,
I'm only surpassed by my intelligence,
for my mistakes there is no penance.
For it is the nature of war,
that I march on for my love.
For it is the patriotism,
that keeps me marching on.

Keep marching on,
for country and state.
Keep marching on,
for death is fate.
Keep marching on,
for bombs come late.
Keep marching on,
forward into time.

Demien Blackthorne

I tried you on,
in forbidden lust.
I left you're side,
you beg to differ?
Hey, now I see you're side,
hid under the malevolent pride,
memories washed aside,
buried deep inside.

Keep marching on,
to death do we die?
Keep marching on,
Keep marching on,
for the lies, lies, lies...

Love's Prayer

———— ∞ ————

He strolled under the moonlit stars.
To him they twinkled so bright that,
he wished that his lover was there with him.
But all he has with him are the memories,
and their late night dip in the seas of bliss.
They danced together like elegant swans,
seeming so happy and content as they danced,
that was as these lovers should be.
But the others are too blinded to see,
that she is the lover for him,
the one and only lover for him.
He may be a dark and mysterious man,
but when he starts think of her,
he's serious about his future plans,
He'd engage her here and now on his knees,
but she's too distant for him to see.
So until she feels the same, he'll start playing his guitar.
Strumming away his own little tunes,
For her, and only her, it's all about her…
and them together…for all of eternity…

Demien Blackthorne

Love Gone

————— ∞ —————

I'm sitting listening to my sanity, that which pours from my radio,
the soothing tune of self destruction, rock and roll in purest form.
Like a mirror on the wall, it reflects me and my life,
all the madness and strife, of the long forgotten night.
When was I told that this is to be? When was I told what to be?
Forever hear the words I long for, forever see the sight I'm searching for.
I'm standing for what I believe is right, but everybody tells me I'm wrong.
What is wrong or right, who is to say? Why couldn't one of them stayed?
Now traveling down the road from a phone call,
my soul mate wanted to speak to me at midnight,
finding out that she loves me, and I am her fate.
It's known what to do, It's known what to say,
I know why I was made, I know why I stay.
What made this life to be? What made the hate inside of me?
Forever hear the words I've prayed for, forever to see the sight I searched for,
forever to see the light of day.

Looking For Someone

———— ∞ ————

(wishes of the white knight)

He wished he could feel
The joys of family life.
Some ones' heart he wants to steal,
So he can have two kids and a wife.
He's looking for someone, to hold him in their arms.
He's looking for someone, to love him for all time.
He sat alone in his bedroom chamber,
listening to the songs of forgotten lore.
Hoping he would be her groom,
and escape his life's monotonous chore.
He's looking for someone, to hold him in their arms.
He's looking for someone, to love him for all time.
Would she ride away with him into the sunset?
and experience the joys of his perfect life?
Would she love and stay with him,
and want become his first wife?
He's looking for someone, pure of heart and trustworthy.
He's looking for someone, with whom to share his imaginary empire.

Little Boy Within

— ∞ —

We were together for a short time,
and though she's not near me right now,
I still feel the deepest love for her ,
even though the distance separates us.
Others have tried breaking my walls,
But they could only scrape the dust.
And she came crashing through,
to save his little boy within.
He only wore that shell of hate,
because it was his security,
the pride of black leather.
But she seen right through his mask,
to his own little boy within himself.
She knows that he's a fragile man,
Whether by wasting time or watching a trial,
He breaks so easily,
When his little boy within
cries…

And when he cries his sorrows,
from drinking the vial of fire water,
the malevolent shell cries out his soul mates name,
revealing the broken man that he's become.
But she pieced him back together,
and wiped his tears away,
with her sweet , innocent voice
promising to always stand by his side.
And his little boy within, full of happiness,
runs through her green fields of joy,
and he's trying to help her catch up
to the wasted shell that left her behind.

Lost and Found

———— ∞ ————

I lost my creation today, trusting the neglected day,
I lost my devotion today, expecting someone would stay,
I lost my lucidity today, reconstructing to course the way,
I found my power today, writing for a new day.
I want to be loved truly, to be loved deeply,
I want to be loved madly, to be loved sincerely,
I need to live life to the fullest, the utmost extent,
but my segregated path is also hell bent.
I've never really loved anyone, because no one really loved me,
all they did was feed the hate that grows inside me,
and rape the man I'm destined to be,
but someday soon they will see.
I found my soul mate today, loving her all the way,
I found my happiness today, Fucking her in every way,
I found out my insanity today, saving it for those who betray,
I lost myself today, falling deeper into the abyss of clay.

Loves Pitfalls

———— ∞ ————

A beauty like no other
and a man of solid integrity.
Sitting together below the starlit sky,
loving each other for all time.
And in this situation they find,
Numerous complexities and agitation's,
even though both vow a feeling of love,
but soon should they triumph over all.
Into this dark void of a mistake he fell,
his emotions reeling from his life's pain,
as he calls her to apologize,
and fix this mess he created.
And in this situation he finds,
an omniscient feeling of love,
and omnipotent determination,
to be with his soul mate lover.
In so doing, their fate is sealed,
forever walking the marital road,
and in his own life she finds,
the one whom would carry her home.

Melody

All I want is the chance, to see millions of my fans,
cheering me on, into the recesses of the night.
All I want is the chance, to give people the ultimate party,
to lift their spirits, and too boldly go beyond.
Running through the wild, I find my own path,
growing out of a child, I unleash my wrath, upon the your world.

The Memory Remains

———— ∞ ————

Why did someone of your stature, tempt him?
How could you draw his eyes away, for another day?
He'd gladly give up all that he has, for her (drugs and music too.)
But the only question in his mind, could he put his trust in you?
Claudia, mirror in vain, you know he's insane,
even with his fortune and fame, the memories will still remain.
He can't see what's going on, around him.
Too many nosey people blind him, to what he believes is true.
If only he could see inside your mind, and know for sure of your intentions.
Maybe then he could choose, whether your his friend or soul mate.
Claudia, mirror in vain, he can feel your pain,
His misfortune is to blame, all his memories stay the same.
Maybe he could walk out, and leave your world behind him in autumns dust.
Leave behind the memories of his blackened past.
But he would be treading unknown territory.
He would need directions to find his way.
Jamie, started the pain
Leona, went a little insane
Even with his fortune and fame
Claudia, these memories still remain.
They tell him whom he should be, and what he should strive to become.
He knows he can be trusted by you, Claudia.
If the chance for him arose he'd be true to you through and through.
Even if some called it a mistake.
With his fortune and fame, he loves her in vain,
but their memories, still remain…

Monotonous

I've been passed up all my misdirected life,
I just couldn't seem to satisfy their vision,
I've lost all my will to live this life,
I need someone to pacify the desire.
I only wanted one thing in this life,
but everyone looked away from the mirror.
I can't love anything or anyone any more,
and you can't get blood out of a dead man.
With all that happens in the world,
what reasons do we have to exist?
I have only had reasons for months at a time,
either betrayed or acting in betrayal.
I guess the only thing that matters is nothing,
'cause if something mattered,
then maybe I'd care about it.
But it seems I have nothing to care about,
since the only things that seemed to care,
are electronically driven by the bullshit fed reels,
of magnetic stripped reproduction equipment.
Vibration of sound enters the mind,
tells me I've been left behind,
tells me what I want to be,
but something holds me back.
Whether it be something from the past,
I do not know. I do not know if I have a soul,
and if I had one, when did I lose it?

I want to be a happy person,
but I can't be happy with myself,
if I'm missing the qualities that make me whole.
I don't even know what I'm missing in myself.
I can't find a reason to live,
the music is just as dull as the drugs,
everything that was fun,
just seems fucking monotonous.

My Life?

———— ∞ ————

Where is my life?
In the feeling of supreme bliss,
in the feeling of achievement,
it's over there with my swiss miss.
What is my life?
The wealth of my fame and fortune,
the pride of this fulfilled person,
it's always been this.
When is my life?
After exiting my mother's womb?
Just before I meet my death?
It's here and now.
I'm hoping that someday soon,
that your love will fill my void,
and that my forgotten self will come back,
and will be remembered as a hero.
Love is a gift, one that should be cherished.
Life is this, right here, and in the now.
Life is the feeling of infinite love,
I live my life only for you.

Myself

———— ∞ ————

I know my forgotten name,
but not my blackened heart.
I know my loving religion,
but not my demented mind.
Yes, I know my forgotten name,
but I can't judge me the same,
because I severed him from my brain
and now he's making me insane.
Don't try to hide the truth from me,
don't try to stifle my dreams,
because we're both the same in the end,
DEAD when we pretend!

Demien Blackthorne

New Rhyme for the Time

——— ∞ ———

I want to be a pokemon, so I can take a pikachu.
If she don't suck, she's out of luck.
Are their mirrors in your pockets, cause I can see myself in your pants.
If she don't spread, I turn my head.
If she don't blow, she'll never know.
Show me some crack, so I can hit the sack.
I suck on the tit and clit, stick the chick a new hot rod,
be a motor god, piston pounding, up inside her,
all warm and moist, lips of choice,
loudened voice in the dead of night,
all out of sight, ex-boyfriend fights,
bright lights, biggest cities,
suck all the girls titty's, chill with fifties,
got gold rings on the fingers, watch the L.A. Lakers,
read about me in the paper, mastermind behind a caper,
not no damn faker, take my shit to heart,
love with open arms, breakfast be lucky charms,
around eight o'clock get up start a new day,
smoke a bowl from yesterday, buy an o z to smoke with Ozzy,
like to watch Fonzi, Saturday morning, get all horny,
from my woman, beauty from Kentucky,
guess I'm lucky, tame as a puppy, wild as a bull, and I shoot to thrill.

Not Worried

———— ∞ ————

Why the fuck should I try to love,
when you fucking bitches look past my frame.
I guess I should hate everyone, kill you all just the same.
You think you know me, but deepest desires I'll never see,
because there are no gods, and wishes don't come free.
So fuck all you whom think I'm not worthy,
cause at the end of this game,
I'll find Diedra and in a blink of an eye,
I'll have courage to have fortune and fame.
But until the destiny of life rides, I'll sit and dream of cascade eyes,
and when the stars are right, I and Cthulu will start a fight.
So in this little revelation at sea, the island will surface in front of me,
and when I step on the forgotten shore, Cthulu will rise forever more!
Stalk the night like an inbred wolf,
and breath deep the steel cloak of night,
remember the last day of your life, the tunnel of light shined so bright.
But now it seems that your dead, and I can forget about my head.
We were bred to suffer and born to die,
much like humans on a sacrificial eve.

Never Mind

I guess I've finally done it,
I've got myself backed in a corner,
I cannot live life without love,
and now I seems I will never find,
never mind…
Never mind the hate, it's always going to be there.
Never mind the lack of will, it's never been there.
Never mind the death of life, it's not worth worrying about.
And never mind about myself, he's been dead for a while.
I guess I have no reason to care,
I'm passed up every time I shine,
so with the insanity in reason and rhyme,
I have found myself to fall behind.
Never mind…
Never mind the war, it's only for awhile.
Never mind the murder, it's only for a smile.
Never mind what peace has to offer, it can't be reached.
Never mind the wound, we all bleed the same.
So I guess that's what I have to say,
about my lonely heart's decay,
No more will to survive,
nothing left in this world for a reason to strive.
Never mind the time, there's never enough of it anyway.
Never mind the crime, we're all still running from the law.
Never mind what we have to say, you wouldn't listen anyway.

Never Say Sunday

———— ∞ ————

Rocking and rolling all night long,
write down the lyrics, sing my song.
Play guitar with the greatest ease,
doing every woman that I please.
Seen the dark side of passion plays,
segregated church confessions on Sundays.

Fine suits, best cigars, war for God.
Wine abuse, neck noose scars, God for war.
Live life blindly…
…Ignorance is bliss.

Driving my car down a lonely dirt road,
flying in home to stay, my only abode.
Knocking my head against a matriarchal wall,
seeing my fate unfold as I slowly fall.
Eleventh moon smiles during night of despair,
still ask myself why "I didn't care".

Broken heart, bitter betrayal, stop the train.
Wounded dove, soulless love, stop the pain.
Resurrected, insurrected, lethal poison injected.
Instruction, destruction, medieval mind infected.
Dead from decay, found a better way today.
Head bomb delay, bound a never say Sunday.

Demien Blackthorne

I tried to tell you about me,
but deaf ears can't hear my plea,
loving you until my end,
regretting that I pretend.
Pretend everything's alright,
my own life so out of sight.

Fine suits, best cigars, war for money
Wine abuse, noose neck scars, money for war,
I won't take anymore.

Unexplainable Feeling

—————— ∞ ——————

I try to hide it by hating everyone,
showing no remorse for the things I've done.
My anger, my sorrow, over what was lost, the anger at myself,
and the sadness for losing love.
I try to hide the suffering of my soul,
which seems to have been torn to pieces,
the fabric savagely ripped apart, by my own two hands.
I killed that which filled me, which gave unto me true life,
the friendship and the love of another,
the one whom I still have deep wounds for.
She was always watching me through the paper masquerade,
reading between lines that weren't there, thinking things that were untrue,
until I gave the reason to believe.
'I don't care anymore' became my choice of phrase,
which made me relive past days, and fall through the cracks of life's maze.
I've fallen so damn far, that I can't see,
but that of the dimmest light which still shines for me.
The candle is burning it's piercing glare,
searing my own essence to mature the solitaire.
The one who still grows since that day, the day when my soul left town.
Now I'm his dominion for his plans, starting off with the rock bands.
Demien Black Thorne, front and center stage,
releasing my God's only rage, of which created his own existence,
the loss of the forgotten female sage.
Now I know why I still love her, now I know why I'd still die for her,
now I know why everything I do is for her,

so I can regain myself, and my soul mate.
But it seems she can't hear me, no matter how loud I yell her name,
Every night it's the same, the one person that I could trust,
floated away with Autumn's dust, I fear now that this is what I must do,
severe the head of he whom laughed at you.
But the sad thing is that, I cannot kill him, I cannot hurt him,
he is what I created to become of me,
so that no one would hurt me ever again.
Now I see that he's working to good, every potential love is cast away,
like a flat skipping stone, bouncing off of the watery glass.
In this glass is a mirror of me and my fate, I see her saying high,
then goodbye, was I really too late?
Or was this part of my fate?
I still love her deep within the recesses of my soul,
even though its dead but dreaming,
dreaming of reuniting together once more,
for the last and final roll of the dice.
This was not my fate.
My fate is to love her forever and a day.
No one will stand in my way.
not anyone in this world, or any other world,
SHE IS MINE!

Oceans

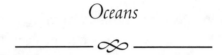

Time flows like a river, and we were merely ships.
Riding with the current, hoping to reach our destinations.
Many storms will pass us by, and try to wreck our fated vessel,
but we must be strong, and push forward through the night.
Many passengers will come our way, some we hope will stay,
but their time comes before ours, as their ship sinks into the endless blue.
Their is no guess work to be had, only decisions based on fact,
sail with more than just wind, sail with knowledge and experience.

Old Highway

———— ∞ ————

Does not the thunder boom, when there is anger in the air?
Or does not the moth fly to the light, when there is death in the air?
Does not the diamond show so crystal clear,
when there is a beauty in my lair?
The time has shown that there's nothing to hide,
as they asphyxiate my last breathe of air.
Dying, I'm on my way down that highway,
flying, on that old highway to hell.
There was no traffic lights, or even a speed limit,
just the wheels of my Cadillac,
turning round and round on the brimstone pavement.
Feeling the wind in my hair, I scream for more,
never really knowing what this life was for.
Speeding, down that old dusty highway.
Laughing, down that old highway to hell.
So I guess I did everything I could of done, never a dull moment for me.
Just kept pushing forward, forward for the line,
mowing them down just to get ahead.
Taking their daily bread, just to get fed, shoot them again, in the head,
life of love and lust and greed, take what it needs to succeed,
no living inbreed, spreading my seed,
hoping the next generation will heed,
to the words I've said, about my head, "But what about the dead?"
The dead are dead, leave them be,
don't ever want to see, the worst side of me,

coming out in happy glee, to destroy thee,
better run, better hide, so that I can't find thee,
pray that you don't end today, I'll find you tomorrow, amidst all this sorrow,
the time I borrow, to bring this all down to you, who like to screw,
who like to chill with weed, and the women who succeed,
chasing the greed,
got hearts that don't bleed, we don't care what you've seen,
or if you smoke the green,
just don't talk, take it to Woodstock,
remains of the faded kiss from the one you miss,
and don't forget about the bliss of sitting with a swiss miss, waiting to
piss, in a war hoping they'll miss, and I guess that's a rap.

Demien Blackthorne

Once Upon a Time

———— ∞ ————

I had a true friend once, she was a good friend too,
but they had a blindness, that wouldn't let me see,
her true identity.
That not only was she a friend, but she was my soul mate too.
So now here I am regretting what I've done, and how I've acted.
Into this ever reaching, endless night, where the stars will see me too,
and the moon had a demented grin, that mocked my every move.
I want to come back, but I don't know if you'll take me,
because I have that wild side, that seems to fuck myself over out of love.
So I'll just say hello, and I'll never say goodbye,
but say unto you...
Until we love again.

One Day

———— ∞ ————

I died one day, only to be reborn in your eyes.
I cried one day, over your shoulder in the skies.
I lied one day, because I felt my happiness threatened.
I sighed one day, when you promised to love me true.
I've done all these things, and your love I will gain.
I'll love you more than life, because you saved me from strife.
If I can win your heart, I might as well try.
If I can't win anyone's heart, then I guess I might as well die.
So remember, I'll love you always, even if you don't feel the same.
I'll find some friends and drugs to forget I changed my heart.

Paid a Quarter

———— ∞ ————

I put my quarter in her hand, she was looking pretty hot,
with her short skirt and long legs, smoking a cigarette like dynamite,
lighting up my night life as she slid over to the juke box,
dropped in my quarter, and played me a live wire,
now I'm sitting in her lust fire.
I started rocking, I started rolling, I started singing like TNT,
I hope she'll notice me, please send your love to me.
I bought her a drink, and talked like a shrink,
and she started to think, that maybe I, was worth her time.
So fuck the golden standards, and fuck the purity prose,
we can fuck the night away, and suck on my six inches.
Cause I'm not a fool, I'm in love with you.

The Past Ends

If it were easy for me to say, I'd live in a forgotten day.
If it were easy for me to tell, I could stop this ring of hell.
But being blind as I am, I can't see the end.
And being mute to a friend, only makes me pretend.
I see myself as a god, being loved by all,
I see myself as a man, standing above it all,
I saw her in the dim twilight of morning,
crying over the loss of my heart and soul.
I saw her in the ring of the moon light,
flying over the land of my lost dreams.
I saw her looking into my bedroom window,
watching me meticulously write my songs.
I saw her wandering down a forgotten road,
wishing she had a way to atone.
But I see it's the end for me, end the dream to be,
end the magick that consumes me.
I'm only a man, a man I cannot stand, I cannot stand alone in the night.
So now that he's gone, and I have left, maybe I did pass my own test?
Someday I'll never know, Someday she will show,
and someday the forgotten wind will blow.
I will be carried away by Autumns dust,
in this life I have no trust.
For these reasons I know I must,
slit the throat of my body,
so that I can finally be free.

Demien Blackthorne

Pseudo-God Shift

———— ∞ ————

I had dreams of leaving this two-bit town, going got nowhere.
Now my dreams have appeared in my life, going got some love.
My dark dreams died with my created evil god
going to throw him a time bomb.
I'm sorry I did it this way, but he hasn't going got to me.
I'm in a living heaven, dream dreams that dream,
I'm in a virtual world, inside certainty I believe.
Power outage for Demien on the eastside,
serve's that mother fucker right.
told the gods to send him to oblivion.
Now I'm cleansed for my main lady,
tokeing jib after bowl. Hit that bong friends.
Heaven is so nice this time of the millenium,
so many souls that did what they please.
I'm living, I hope you see me soon,
achieving my dreams with your love beside me.
My soul has been emancipated by
the one friend who helped me stop the trend.
I never followed anyone or anything,
I made my own decisions, whether right or wrong.
I paid a price for the wrong,

and reaped rewards for the right.
But now everything is white as snow,
and I can see everything.
Heaven and Hell are lies,
God and Satan are fictional,
inside this "loving" god's eyes,
everyone will realize.

Demien Blackthorne

Portrayal

———— ∞ ————

His way was in his eyes, devil's disguise,
His day was in his skies, hallowed God lies,
Our life was made from dust,
in faith can we trust?
Our body's are his servants,
in slavery cuffs.
My way was in my friends, bitter dead ends,
May day is that of the dead, path I tread.

My life is nothing,
my soul is something,
My insanity is shining,
my work is clever spying.

My looks are in overdrive, passion prowler.
My faces are in a muff dive, massage parlor.
Our sex was life's must,
in love can we trust?
My body is you're servant,
in doubt I wander.
You're ways are deceitful, forked tongue lethal,
You're lies are betrayal, caused hell's portrayal.

You're life is something,
You're soul is crying.
You're insanity is becoming,
You're scream is deafening.

Prologue

———— ∞ ————

I've been thinking about us
You and me…
Together…

Happiness always seemed to elude me,
But somehow I've grasped it.
I have the diamond in my hand;
I carry it across the land.
It shines brighter than any star.
The land of Eden is not far.
You're just a stones throw away.
I think of you night and day.
I'd fight to the death,
Just to be with you.
I love you in so many countless ways.
I'll be there, always.
Protecting you from countless things;
Going to see you on golden wings.
I'll always be there,
Loving you until the end.
The wounds in my heart are no longer here,
You were the only one who could heal them.
You're just a stones throw away.
I think of you night and day.
I'd fight to the death,
just to be with you.

Pressure Release

I'm in my own little world,
that which is in my mind at night,
for it is the only place in town,
where I were a crown.
I have so many choices,
from the women I've seen,
they all love me in my mind,
the only place that's safe for me.

I dream about faded kisses,
pressure release.
I dream about jaded misses,
pressure release.
In the dead of night,
everything comes out right.

They all love me, every single one,
no judgment calls or rocky falls,
just the rapture of sweaty skin,
and the seven shot gin from a girl named Kim.
Last time I got laid in reality,
she bit me on the neck,
I know I'm going to die some day,
but where's the fuck?!

Demien Blackthorne

I dream of wet pussy lips,
pressure release.
I dream of pointed fingertips,
pressure release.
If it wasn't for the dream,
the women in reality would scream.

Reasons

———— ∞ ————

At this point in time, I am alone.
But I have someone, waiting for me.
All this time, I've known.
You were meant for me.
The first indication of this,
your "Silent Lucidity".
It played on the radio, that angelic night.
I slept in your arms, feeling complete.
Hoping that some day, we'd see the altar.
This memory replays for me, the happiest day.
I relive it every night, everyday.
Being happy, then opening my eyes,
to the emptiness of this room, I cry.
Waiting was the hardest part,
Counting down the days was the easiest.
All this is worth it,
to see her in that white gown.

The Road I Traveled

I know what to do now, burn up all of life's energy,
upon the stage in town, and the giving of sympathy.
Once I find myself, I'll be loving what I find,
discarding my last self, and leaving any trace of hate behind.
So, she's always at my abode, reading poems, loving me all the way,
stopping at friends abodes, tokeing jibs and drinking lodes.
Memories die in my mind in time, through reason and Rhyme,
I will find what I desire to be mine, the succulent loins of a loving bride.

Rock & Roll Band

———— ∞ ————

Well, we're not really quiet,
and we're not really quaint,
so don't try to fight it,
cause we'll beat you into it .
work our fingers to bone,
for minimum wage rage,
stuck in an iron cage,
we became big time stars.

It was a long time,
before we could rock and roll.
It was a chance we took,
to start our rock and roll.

parents don't understand,
that we have to play it loud,
our friends don't believe us,
that we would get this far.
But don't tell them we did.

It was a long time,
before we could rock and roll.
It was every chance we took,
to be able to rock and roll.

Demien Blackthorne

We've got the time,
We've got the money,
We've got the song,
to make you our honeys.
So take a trip with us,
to uncensored x t c,
and don't worry about me,
I'm getting high with ma boys.

Diedra of the Garden

I'll never leave her behind,
she loves even my darkest kind.
In her blue eyes lie the depths,
of my own soul waiting for release.
All those around me oppose the union,
but they do not know what I do.
I know more than they are thinking,
I'm about to start sinking.
Sinking back into my life of only for her,
even if my friends disagree.
After they see us together,
they'll see a new side of me.
The side I never showed to the world,
for the world doesn't deserve me.
But in the reality sense,
she deserves me more than I her.
All these so called friends are hurting me,
directing me to a different path,
but I know what I want,
I want the carnation,
That Diedra of the garden holds for me.

School

———— ∞ ————

My classes suck, my teachers hate me.
No work is done, all for fun.
They bore me to, the edge of death.
Waiting for the bus, exhaling icy cold breath.
Working on cars, first and second,
History scores in third, and Geometry in the fourth dimension.
R.A.P. Rides fifth, English 10 sixth and last.
When I'm home, I'll have a blast.
Sleeping now and then, uh-oh, detention again.
From three to three-thirty, picking up the lazy trash.
Weekends are a blur, for I am not sure,
where to begin, on how to win.

Self-Slavery

———— ∞ ————

I'm a slave for mischievous intentions,
They all hollowed out my apprehensions.
She came in like a specter apparition,
beckoning my morbid parturition.
Divided by the souls of the slain,
living out their constant pain.
Now that I think of that starlit night,
I'm ready and willing to take flight.
Into death we die, into mists we ride.
Into truth we lie, only to stay satisfied.
A warm glow from months past,
my ale lager never could last,
stretching my arms out forth,
only to be made into morph.
Alternating Chameleon in my blood,
as my legs are sinking in mud.
All I ask is leave me be,
don't search for the demons inside me.
Into the bed I sleep, wooden planks that creek,
slain like first born sheep, my soul sinks into the deep.

Self Instruction

———— ∞ ————

Self instruction of the damned, legions of the mindless scammed,
classes in the college crammed, self instruction of the damned.
Self destruction of the lamb, bury their heads in the sand,
of a poisoned radioactive land, self destruction of the lamb.
Self concentration of the man, living by a books master plan,
churches pass the can of scam, self concentration of the man.
Self indignation of the clan, provoking the violence planned,
crushing the bones underfoot, self indignation of the clan.
Self extinction of the race, living in tormented disgrace,
boxed in a cold dark place, self extinction of the race.

Screaming for the End

— ∞ —

My dead body was dreaming, and you woke up screaming,
hoping for monotonous joy, I became your little toy.
My lifeless body was leaning, and you kept on learning,
about my gross abomination, for their hopeless extermination
Screaming for the end, I was your only friend.
Screaming for the end, why should we pretend.
Your frivolous excitation, was the only explanation,
for the sins I endure, come, give me the CURE!
Your insatiable lust, fed my only hunger,
and now that I can trust, I wish I was your lover.
Screaming for the end, I've found my only friend,
Screaming for the end, my soul mate is around the bend.
I believe in your love for me, to end my ring of irony,
to fly to you like a dove, to my only destiny,
my soul mate.

Second Chance

———— ∞ ————

Love is in the air, and you're the one I'm thinking of.
You know I care, for my only dove.
She has given me a chance, to be happy again.
She has taken the lance, out of my heart again.
She gives me her love, and mine to share.
I'm free as a dove, in the midnight air.
I'm flying to a place, that is full of light.
I see her face, so beautiful in the night.
You make me who I am, you are whom I see holding my hand,
and we, together, love for all time, and we last a lifetime.

Soulless Dead

---∞---

I seem to have lost my soul, like I signed my own death warrant.
Just because of someone I knew, that turned the other cheek.
I gave up my sanity, pride, and mind,
all because someone led me to believe.
So I went along for the ride, shedding the insecurity that I hide.
War alive louder than before.
Evil takes it's toll all the more.
Fight for what's right in the heart, somewhere there's got to be a start.
He created a God for me to worship, blood, sweat, and steel.
(Arrow, Sulfur, and Sword).
Gave up my will to survive, wild and crazy man revived.
AC/DC running through the veins, heart pumping the brain insane.
Overheating my solid emotions, I dream of new devotions.
Peace thrive prouder than the lore, of Ancient Gods and forgotten gore.
Light your own flight in the dark, just like Lucifer dancing in the park.
Now that it's all done and said…
I can forget about the soulless dead.

Demien Blackthorne

Song of a Life Not Lived

————— ∞ —————

Life is a song, full of high and low tones.
It doesn't matter if their right or wrong,
because in the end, they're just dust'n'bones.
There was a young man on the hill, with mountains of money.
A wild woman gave him a thrill, the scent of her sassafras honey.
And this was the woman, who lived down the lane.
She loved that man with all her heart and soul,
that she invited him over to her abode.
And now laying on her bed, he sees her as his soul mate,
and now they will be wed, after he finishes his literary work.

Something Unexplained

I took a walk around my world,
to ease my troubled time.
I watched my world go through,
the dark side of my tomb.
Will I die tonight?

It's not for me to be dead,
but I stumbled into life.
Left all I loved behind the wall,
awaiting night's deadly fall.
Will I fry tonight?

If I went crazy, would I still be sane?
If I went home, would I still be bumming.

Fun and fill, weasel thrill,
a buddy that doesn't exist.
Demien running up in the mist,
waking up the dead from the hill.

Demien Blackthorne

From the depth's of a forgotten life,
he surfaced to hunt the shadows.
Not knowing what his only mission was,
he marched forward for his own unholy cause.
Crawling chaos, cult has summoned,
depths underground, twisted sound.
Sacred sleep, has been upset,
he awakened, dawning of a new age rising.

Face the one that should not see,
face the one that should not live.
In mental anxiety he fell.

Standing Alone

There is a place where the willow trees grow,
This is the place I like to go.
Where whisper thin winds blow across a desolate land,
and where my heart is in her hand.
The grassy fields play all day, while I walk the lonely stray,
wondering what might have been, wishing for what is now past.
My heart helps the trees grow, my mind makes the wind blow,
and my pitiful sorrow, brings gentle rains of yore.
Memories washed away by slowly passing time,
trying to forget life's monotonous rhyme,
hoping someday I'll find, someone who can truly be mine.

Demien Blackthorne

SUICIDE

My life exploded today and everyone hated me then,
now they have no idea what to believe.
I fluctuate between happiness and sadness.
Remembering those I lost hoping for those I've won.
No one knows my sadness in it's infinite void.
Falling through chaos looking for a way to escape.

My life exploded today
Blood and brains on the floor
No one knows my depression
It's something I never shared
Something that had no expression
Except for a trigger happy hand
And every fucked up part of my existence
FIXXXED
In one determined moment
When all aspects of life
Ceased to exist

Sweet Memory

————— ∞ —————

What I once thought was back in the past,
has come to help me last.
Like a dream woven of fantasy,
you waded into my life's mess.
I awoke from a startling dream,
Frightened in cold sweat.
As we danced there under the moonlight,
my mind wandered in happiness.

Then I thought of what I wanted,
Next I thought of what I really needed,
I wanted to dance with the sacred flame,
the only love for me.

Ignorance helped the better of me,
arrogance plagued the lesser of me,
and I found what really mattered to me.
My love, my life, and what once lived in me.

All roads in life, lead somewhere,
but I see the road to your lair.
I remember that of the sacred kiss,
in my deepest memory.
She once played a song for me,
deepest dreams and hopes I see,
"Turn the Page", and you will see,
My own soul is alive inside of me.

Demien Blackthorne

I thought of what I enjoyed,
I thought of what I really needed,
I needed to feel the arms,
of my sweet, sweet memory.

The sweet memory, of my fate to be,
with the only one whom loved me.

The Last Poem of Jazz

Demien Black Thorne is dead, no doubt about it,
his demise,
wearing a two faced disguise.

Once shed from his host's life, he fell back to whence he came,
his own prison,
the Nexxus he created for him and Diedra.

They are both in the Nexxus, loving for eternity,
his own mission,
finished after his host saw him truly.

The host left empty and for the dead, found a God more worthy,
Jazz White Thorne,
the only God that reflected his heart.

Now Jazz must find his lover and consort, the one so true,
her name unknown,
until she came up and into the real house of Jazz.

Once she enters, she'll never look back, and she'll know,
this was meant to be,
because Jazz is the only one who could see.

Demien Blackthorne

The world becomes perfect when they meet, perfect love,
created for them,
so that they can live for eternity in the lake of bliss.

Now that things have finished their course, with no remorse,
Love lives eternally,
on the earth with no hate to plague it ever again.

The Wait

—— ∞ ——

Left alone by myself, I wait.
Hoping for what might be, I wait.
Dreaming dreams only I can dream, I wait.
To be hers once more, I wait.
Wondering about my future, I wait.
Sitting in a dark desolate place, I wait.
I wait, and I wait.
What is to become of my fate?
To be alone forever,
or just to be hers evermore?
I wait for you, to make your choice.
I wait for you, to hear your voice.
I wait for me, to not be so blind.
I wait for me, as I walk one step behind.
I wait for us to be together.
I wait for us to be forever.
I wait, and I wait.
What is to become of my fate?
To die alone?
Or to be perched next to her throne?
Go where you must, I'll wait.
Be with whom you wish, I'll wait.
Be with him or me, I'll wait.
Am I too blind to see, my own fate?
I'll wait for you, until the end of time.
I'll wait for you, in my darkest kind.

Demien Blackthorne

Goodbye, farewell,
I'll wait for you, while I walk through this hell.
I wait and I wait.
What is to become of my fate?
To wait forever and never see what could be?
Waiting was never meant for me.
That's why I helped you see.
The calm ocean of love you have for me.

Thoughts

———— ∞ ————

If it were not for the sands of time,
I could be frozen in the happiest moments of my life.
My heart is that of a chameleon, it changes its color to fit the occasion.
Drowning in an ocean of sorrow, only one person can save me.
My pit's so fucking deep, only one ray of light shows through.
And I am left to wonder, who is shining the light for me.
The goddess in my life?
Or the life of my goddess?
But to who my goddess is, only the sands of time will tell,
and they don't tell me much, for they are as empty as my bottomless heart.
And my mind its to full of menacing memories, that tear at very existence.
The soul has no bounds, but it does have a bond to another,
which is found in the sands of time,
before the bitter end of my darkened days.
Someone true enough to share my life, destined to find her close to home.

Treasures

———— ∞ ————

I crawled up inside it, all warm and moist.
I took a taste of it, parting the lips of choice.
It cooed at the pleasure, fantasies uncensored.
It was my favorite treasure, a rod of steel, black leathered.
Hearts swimming in a lake of bliss, hand cuffs, whips, and chains.
She is someone I'll always have, meeting of these fated souls.
Now she's here, forever to be seen with me,
shall she be the soul mate of my life?
Someone is my true love, that's why I wrote this rhyme.

Trinities End

————— ∞ —————

The death of his strife, occurs over at his soul mates abode.
The stone heart breaks to reveal the gold and when you start to bother him,
about your past troubles with his new found love,
you make the wound she healed, reopen.
He needs no help with problems of yore, the past is past, and dust to dust,
life to him is a fun ride, only love him if you feel, that you're his soul mate.
He's had pain before the trinities end, and someone should know his sorrow,
for when she finds his wounds have healed, then she takes him as her own.
Let him live his way, even if it's with your old flame.
after his debts are paid, you will lie back in the chair of life.

Demien Blackthorne

Tripping to the Other Side of my Mind.

Tripping to the other side of my mind,
I've been around the city block a couple of times,
always rewrite the rhymes, known for infamous crimes, and a shell that
always shines, and keeps still to hide,
myself tripping to the other side of my mind.
seen the ugly side of bad, and the beautiful of whom are empty.
I've also seen the worse of the ugly, go down in flames,
into a black sheet of beautiful emptiness.
While tripping to the other side of my mind.
White woven strands begin to tow the line,
I always step aside every single time I'm forced to regression,
just to keep a hold of what I thought was my pride of oppression,
and in some instances between the spaces of time, I have lied,
While tripping to the other side of my mind.
But my truest intentions are unknown to me, and my spiritual cohorts,
for I even out fox my selves at certain times,
and all that I cherish falls in an abyss of regret.
After tripping to the other side of my mind.
For I loved her an eternity and a day that dawned to spread,
throughout the hallways of my head, of which are dead,
and forgotten for the sake of my sanity deprived life.
Her maiden name rhymes and passes the test,
but it was I that died that day in her chest.
I said my heart stop beating, she said she was cheating,
I find myself repeating the same mistakes,
looking for the goddess in my lake of life,

always run from the strife, only to save my life.
Bitter dead torment for my segregated sins of schizophrenia,
paranoia my closest friend so close to the end,
all the while I wait in the darkness of dementia,
for the unworthy to show themselves to light,
and that's why I continue the illusionary fight.
For my disillusioned world of clouded sight,
I will forever hide in the depths of the nightshade.
Frayed ends of sanity my last choice of phrase,
as I mark out every ones graves,
after the teenage raves, all in the salad days, we'd call ourselves slaves,
but didn't know about the senseless acts,
which makes history retract inside of me,
don't want nobody to know the good side of me,
because the bad makes the soul unclean,
virtually obscene, smoke greeny green,
drop the top AC/id/DC, look for a new team, and a new dream,
died from overdosing on Mr. Clean, found out heaven's just a dream,
one we can't grasp, no matter how long we last.
I know I'm moving to fast,
can't remember who was last, fatal car crash, last episode of MASH,
toke the green grass, sip and chill wit' Velvet, I wear a diamond heart helmet,
that helps me forget, what I am, and who I am, never been caught in a scam,
but maybe a Dodge Ram, came in to slam, my Uncle Sam, last rights
given to the dead, that lay upon my bed, morbid destruction of the flesh,
brings the pleasure of a caress,
like death's sweet lips, kissing my ass goodbye, frying my mind over sin,
sugar coat it with gin, lost the life of a limb, cuss out the worded whim,
I'll kick you in the fucking shin, then push you down the stair rim,
shine the light in your eyes, to expose your lies,

and to resurrect my malicious display, of an affectionate blood spray,
on the eve of revelation, won't practice master nation, cut down on the
fucking inflation, of my head in the skies, reading bible lies, listen to
bullshitting guys,
who tell the Biggie lies, and practice purity in disguise.
All while tripping on the other side of my mind.

Unfinished Life

———— ∞ ————

I know who I am, I just wasn't able to accept him.
In certain ways he scares me, being a push over.
So I made one unlike me, the opposite self.
He made me feel dead alive, that's why I strive.
All those who do know me, know that the shell is a defense.
And when I get in the anamotical stage, he's my offense.
If it wasn't for my open mind, some of them I'd leave behind,
only for one simple fact, the interruption of life and liberty.
But now I see a different side, the one that I am.
Now I have no choice, be who I truly am, as much as it kills the darker,
the one that I have clung to for so long, so damn long.
Four years in the making, lost in the celestial drift of sensible things.
He grew way before my light ever showed, dimming intensity,
blackest heart scarred me still, dead to the world,
now that I'm alive I don't know what to do, indecision.
So many women that plague my sensibility of finding my soul mate,
to who she is I'll never know till she shows, when the wind blows,
and if I should die before I rest, I'll know that I past my test,
and put the butt puppets to rest, all for this noble crest.
A life of liberty laid to waste, all lost in a forgotten place,
time has no meaning as my head is an empty space.

Vaseline

———— ∞ ————

"Can't fuck the fucker
'cause he done fucked you over,
no Vaseline."

I am in your head, it's where I tread, thoughts too wild to express,
it's your fault for this mess. I went along for the ride,
now you can no longer hide,
my rage finds you on the street, trying to sell a pair of keet. You look
and wonder why, you could never touch the sky,
but you could always be the one who fell,
deep into the recesses of my proverbial hell.
Now listen children with open ears,
I'm here to chase away your fears, don't be afraid of what's not there,
'cause chances are you'll find it everywhere. Tread the unmarked road like
a beaten path, you never could understand the math,
1+1=3, but you know it was me.
It was me and I am loved by you, It was always you!
You were always loved by me, Crawled back out from under a rock,
the sunlight gave me an electric shock,
I looked up toward the sky only to see,
that the storm clouds of love were engulfing me.
Shocked to see my own life so true,
that I found someone special and new,
she lifted me up to the highest skies, filling my heart with her love.
Riding on cloud number nine, I drink to 'Strawberry Wine',
knowing full well that my dark side has died,

I'm asking my chosen God why He even lied.
It was me and I was too angry to see, that he wasn't out to hurt me.
"He couldn't except the decision I made, so I told him he was jealous.
And if you ask me, I'll tell you too, that I'll always love you"
Now that he's out of our way you could start to love me,
and in my truest and only sense, I know our love will recommence.

Demien Blackthorne

"Waiting"

I was being an uncle to my nieces over spring break.
We watched movies, played with toys, and to me, this was one of life's joys.
I felt like a father, and it felt good, letting them help with dishes.
They slept so content at nap time, and I know that I am a good father.
So why can't I have a family of my own.
Because the years spread us apart and the law creates walls.
I enjoy watching my nieces, and I can't wait until I have my own little angels.
But until then, I'll sit and dream, of our family.
I'll sit and wait for our wedding, wait for our love to bloom.
Because in time I know very deeply I'll have my family…With you.

Watching My Every Step

Through the good times, and the bad, and all the sorrow I've had,
you were there, watching my every step.
I don't know how to thank you, you've shown me so much,
yet, I gave so little, and still, you stayed.
I'm caught between the celestial rift, limbo between life and death,
but you were there, to keep me in check.
Through the good times, and the bad, all the sorrow I've had,
you were there, watching my every step.
No amount of wealth could out weigh my love,
nor could any power draw me away, I'm always yours.
Here we are above the world on the wings of love.
There is nothing we fear, because we are together.
And through the mists of time, our love will last forever.
We will be together, for all eternity.
Through the good times, and the bad, after all the sorrow I've had,
you were there, solid as a rock, and soft to the touch,
watching my every step.

Demien Blackthorne

Way Life Was Writ

I keep trying to release myself from the pain,
but no one can wash away the stain.
The illicit drugs only pacify the hurt for awhile,
and in the state of perpetual sluggishness I smile.
I like to consider myself dead as a door nail,
a corpse for your new world resolutions.
I bleed for the consecration of my sinister style,
death seems like the final solution to my pollution.

My heads in a trip,
I'll take a little sip,
crack the leather whip,
the way my life was writ.

Standing idly by, while all the others fly,
living my life without love I suffocate myself.
Every woman I know walks on by,
why can't the world just let me die.
I revel in the gothicism of living dead,
I believe I'm immortal, an unliving soul.
And in the distant future I can see,
there will be no resurrection for me.

My heads in a trip,
I only took a little sip,
being choked by a whip,
this life has turned to shit.

Maybe this is my life by my design,
scrape and form a little white line.
When I'm drugged, I'm in the Aleysian fields,
so out of the world scene, the world schemes,
and my last digit in life lets out a deadly scream.
I'm happy to die alone and forgotten,
the prophesies on my life are true.

My heads in a depression trip,
I dementedly took a little sip,
choked myself out of life,
it's true, I've created my own strife.

Demien Blackthorne

Wedding Vows

———— ∞ ————

I need you(to help build my empire)
I want you(to be my queen)
I need you(in my life)
I want you(to be my wife)

So many questions concern us.
Can we trust one another?
So many problems plague us.
Can we be honest to each other?

I love you(truly, madly, deeply)
I love you(with all my heart)
I trust you(in every way)
I trust you(with all my soul)

So many temptations in our lives.
Can we trust one another?
So many systems are in our way.
Can we be honest to each other?

How do you feel(I love you)
Why do we steal(we need to)
Can I trust you(yes)
Can I be honest(yes)

So many years have gone by.
WE TRUST EACH OTHER.
So many tears in our eye.
WE ARE HONEST TO EACH OTHER.

WE ARE HAPPY AND FREE

Demien Blackthorne

What I Must Do

The fire burns bright, almost silent in the night,
blinded by this light, I'm almost losing sight.
The fire is my heart, broken, battered, and betrayed,
to far beyond repair, but then…
I met someone
She made me feel so loved, then she told me to hush,
and I lied to a friend, now there is no pretend.
I know what I have to do, shed the scared little boy,
and take a chance, for I have so much to gain,
and almost nothing to lose.
I want to be by your side, help you ride the tide,
so many times I've died, only you do I confide.

What it means

———— ∞ ————

It says, "Pick me up and lead me, to the pure waters of love,
to the green pastures of sacrifice, and past the edge of forever."
It says, "I hang in the balance, between life and death,
between love and hate, and between legs that go nowhere."
It says, "Lead me to my life, where laughter is accompanied,
where sadness is comforted, and where I am truly happy."
It calls to everyone, who is void of feeling.
Because I myself, am an empty thing.
It calls to anyone, who is willing to fill my soul,
because it is as empty as my bottomless heart.

Demien Blackthorne

Where Am I?

———— ∞ ————

What's wrong with this picture?
Why is my life this way?
Do I ask too much?
Or do I give too little?

I know I dream impossible things.
I can someday be really happy.
I see things in a different light.
That's why I must know.

I'm kidding myself if I say goodbye,
yes, I am absolutely happy here.
And I can hear and see you,
and I want to love you always.

Locked in this cage of doubt,
I'm wondering where I truly am.
The Elysian fields…
Or my own dream?

Why Exist?

———— ∞ ————

Death is only the beginning, of the life that was,
the life that had no meaning, the life that had no course.
Sealed in it's bosom, the hate of the world,
which rose from the abyss, to consume those of immoral hearts.
Hate filled with terror, terror filled with teeth,
teeth bloodied from enemies, enemies destroyed at the stroke of a hand.
It knew not what it was, only that it hated its own existence,
forever trapped in itself, with no escape in sight.
It could think, it could reason, but it could not understand,
that the only reason it was created, was to create.
Hate filled with terror, terror filled my heart,
my heart I gave unto my friends,
my 'friends' destroyed at the stroke of a hand,
destroyed at the stroke of my hand.
All alone, like that of the universe, one single body that only knew hate,
that only knew it existed, that only knew it hated its existence.
And it hated, because it didn't know why, it existed.
It existed to be my friend, and my friend it shall be.

Wishing

———— ∞ ————

I'm sitting with my niece, wishing and wanting desperately,
to be a family man, while we sit and watch peter pan.
Children are sweet and innocent, only until they see the world.
It is only then do they change, and we as parents must rearrange our lives…

They grow up like us in their own way, do almost the same things we did,
some are better, some are worse, and all we can do is hope for the best.
When our children fall we must help them back up,
but there comes a time, when they must pick up themselves.
My three year old niece helped me with dishes,
she washed a plastic measuring cup.
The joy on her face for letting her help,
said to me, "Thank you for this chance."
And we must give all our children a chance,
and no matter what the outcome,
we must be supportive, for if they lose that support,
then they won't be there…
For their own kids.

Waiting for You

I have nothing to lose, except my sanity.
Which I think I've already lost, along with my pity.
I have so much to gain, being with you.
No longer do I feel the pain, because of my love for you.
My feelings for you, get stronger every day.
If it wasn't for you, I'd probably decay.
I'll make my move, when your in the mood.
But until that time, I'll be just fine.
And when you come unto me the third time,
I will be the one you love for all time.

About the Author

I was born in Charlotte, Michigan in 1979. As 2001 approaches, I am close to turning 22. I look out into the world and present things as I see them. All these poems are the truth of the things that have happened to me. If you can cut through the maze like writing you'll be able to see just what I think about love, religion, government, hate, racism, and all the other things that seem to plague a human's life. All human's really want is to be happy and with out worry. We'd like to escape death and watch the world unfold throughout time, but that is only a dream that we cannot have. Too many people hide behind God's promise of everlasting life after death, and rest assured these things I know, for your journey to shall end six feet below. I love to hate this world and the hypocritical Christians that created and control it. That is the main reason for my writing, we all judge each other every day, and I'm tired of being judged. I know my writing has a lot of swearing in it, but those words are in the dictionary, and I believe I have used them to my advantage. If they weren't in the dictionary, nobody would know of their existence, and nobody would use them so easily. A lot of people think drugs are a problem, but really their not. It's the fact that the government has outlawed them that makes them so dangerous. If they were legal, these people wouldn't get shot for narcing out people because there would be nobody to narc out. My personal opinion is that the drugs have actually helped me with my writing, tearing down the walls which I've built over the years. This world is heading for a revolution, and I will be happy to sit back and watch all of you who oppress the human's animal nature burn from your own weapons of mass destruction. Truly, humans are too smart for their own good.

Made in the USA
San Bernardino, CA
18 September 2014